T0352305

ESTATE ACCOUNTS

ESTATE ACCOUNTS

BY

C. S. ORWIN

AND

H. W. KERSEY

Second edition, revised

CAMBRIDGE
AT THE UNIVERSITY PRESS
1936

CAMBRIDGE
UNIVERSITY PRESS

University Printing House, Cambridge CB2 8BS, United Kingdom

Cambridge University Press is part of the University of Cambridge.

It furthers the University's mission by disseminating knowledge in the pursuit of
education, learning and research at the highest international levels of excellence.

www.cambridge.org
Information on this title: www.cambridge.org/9781316603345

© Cambridge University Press 1936

First edition 1926
Second edition, revised 1936
First paperback edition 2016

A catalogue record for this publication is available from the British Library

ISBN 978-1-316-60334-5 Paperback

PREFACE

THE need for accurate accountancy in estate management is fully realised to-day, although it is probable that more use still might be made of book-keeping as an aid to efficiency. By the simple expedient of the arrangement and analysis of the accounts which every land agent keeps, his books will give him at sight details of costs and returns which are not available in a mere summary account without much laborious extraction. If recorded in the appropriate columns of an analysed ledger account, all details of expenditure and the results of financial administration can be subjected to a check and a review, year by year, in a way which has been proved by practical experience to be of real value to the land agent and to his principal, particularly in times like the present, when estate finance is often a difficult problem, and the cost and the value of every item of expenditure must be considered.

The examples given in the pages following are arranged with the object of keeping both landlord and agent posted in the progress of management, receipts and payments being classified and analysed so as to provide essential information at a glance, and without the necessity of further extraction. No attempt has been made to teach the fundamental principles of book-keeping; familiarity with them on the part of the reader is assumed. Nor are the examples of methods necessarily the best in all circumstances, and they are put forward as much to stimulate consideration as for adoption and use as they stand.

C. S. O.
H. W. K.

January 1936

CONTENTS

CHAPTER I

INTRODUCTION

BOOK-KEEPING makes little appeal to the practical man. He has been accustomed to exercise his organising ability and his managerial functions much more by instinct and with the test only of a general result. But in these days the importance of scientific control which can only be secured from accurate and well-planned accountancy is becoming more and more recognised. On many estates the work of the agent is too extensive to enable him to keep under his own eye the conduct of the work for which he has to pay, and, moreover, he is usually equipped with clerical assistance more or less skilled. The controllers of "big business" are rarely technical experts in the work of the enterprises they are called upon to direct. Thus, the Managing Director of Messrs Lyons is not selected for his light hand at pastry, nor is it necessary that the General Manager of the Great Western Railway should be a capable stoker. Men engaged in such capacities rely upon scientific book-keeping for the control of technical management, and the large estate resembles closely the big industrial enterprise in its need for means of financial control, even though it may still be true of the little venture that the master can be engaged more profitably in supervision in the field or in the yard than in the compilation of records and statistics in his office.

A system of estate book-keeping properly designed should serve two purposes; it should enable the agent to account accurately and intelligibly for the money he has received and spent on behalf of his principal, and it should supply information alike to the principal and to the agent which will assist them in the wise administration of the property. The former function of estate accountancy is universally recognised, but it is not so generally realised that information is contained between the covers of an estate ledger by which, when systematically analysed, the development of the property may be controlled. It should not be considered sufficient to be able to present a statement at the close of the financial year showing the receipts and payments recorded under various heads, and the net balance available for the landlord's privy purse. This information is, of course, of prime importance, but by careful arrangement and analysis much more than this can be extracted from the records. It will be within the memory of some that when provision was first made, in the year 1910, to refund to landowners income tax in respect of income laid out on maintenance of property in excess of the statutory allowances, a very small proportion of the amount budgeted for by the Chancellor of the Exchequer was claimed during the following year or two because comparatively few estate offices kept books in a form which would provide the information needed to substantiate a claim. Accounts, properly planned, should furnish particulars of this nature almost at a glance. At the same time they should enable the landlord and the agent to exercise control over the expenditure in various departments of the estate by directing their attention to the changes, year by year, in each. Not only should any increase in total expenditure, say on repairs, be brought out, but the records kept should indicate in what branch of this part of the upkeep of the estate any abnormal outlay had been incurred, and the holding, or holdings, where the work was done. Not only is it important to keep a check on the expenditure in general, but as tenants vary in the nature and in the extent of the demands which they make upon the estate for repairs and new works, good estate management requires that some ready means should be furnished for recording the work done on each holding, and the estate books and the records incidental thereto are the most satisfactory and reliable medium.

This applies in nearly all the departments of the estate. The woodlands may show approximately the same net balance in two years, but the accounts should show, without further analysis, whether this is due to the carrying on of the same policy, or whether exceptional receipts from fellings have been balanced by exceptional expenditure on planting. Again, the advantage or otherwise of raising trees in the estate nursery, as compared with the purchase of trees from a public nurseryman, will emerge from well-kept accounts; the cost of an estate building staff as compared with contract labour; the rise in the burdens on the land due to the changes in taxation, in tithe rent charges, and so on; all these and many other things of interest and of value to those responsible for the management of property, whether as principals or as agents, should be available by reference to the estate books without further analysis or calculation. It is impossible to enumerate them all here, and the information to be gathered will vary from estate to estate, but it should always be borne in mind that the object of estate accountancy is to assist in management, and not merely to vindicate the honesty of those responsible to the landlord for the conduct of his business.

The form in which his estate accounts are kept is a matter which should engage the serious attention of the land agent from time to time. No form is best in all circumstances and for all time. Changes in legislation, changes in the policy of the owner towards his property, may compel an adaptation of existing book-keeping methods to meet the new conditions; but, apart from this, it is worth while always to consider the year's accounts, on the completion of the annual audit, from the point of view of the information they provide for owner and agent alike, and to think whether modifications of existing practice can be introduced which might result in an increase of efficiency in future management.

The system of estate book-keeping described in the following pages is one that will meet the needs of most agricultural estates, whilst it can be adapted without difficulty to special cases. It has been tested in operation, and it was designed so as to entail the minimum of clerical work compatible with the maximum of information on the progress of management.

CHAPTER II

DESCRIPTION OF THE ACCOUNT BOOKS REQUIRED

ESTATE accounts are kept, usually, on the basis of Income and Expenditure. It is neither necessary, customary nor desirable to take account of the Capital invested in the property. Indeed, the capital value is rarely known, and so much of that which might be regarded as capital expenditure, from year to year, represents no more than the replacement of wasting assets. Thus, any attempt to arrive at an initial figure, and then to add to it, or to subtract from it, according as money is laid out, or as assets depreciate, would only involve the accountant in a maze of figures having no substantial basis.

Cash Book. It follows that the primary account book to be kept is the *Cash Book*. Any standard form can be employed that is big enough to provide space on each side for columns as follows: Date of transaction; Particulars of receipt or payment; Name of Ledger account to which the transaction belongs; Folio of appropriate Ledger account; Money column for details of composite receipts or payments; a second money column for the total amount of each receipt or payment. The Cash Book ruled in this way appears on the page opposite.

All receipts and payments, whatever their nature, should be entered in this book. No separate money columns are provided for cash, as distinct from cheques, because it is intended that *all receipts, in either form, should be paid into the bank, and that all payments should be made by cheque*; payments required in cash, such as wages, are made by cheques drawn for the requisite amounts and cashed. Adherence to this practice simplifies the book-keeping, and eliminates the liability to errors which may arise where cash takings are kept in the estate office or in the hands of the subordinates who receive them, and are used to make cash payments. Kept in this way, the Cash Book will always correspond with the bank pass book; the two should be agreed

Cash Book

Receipts

Date	Particulars	Ledger Fo.	£	s	d	£	s	d
1934 Jan 1	To Owner Cash Advanced — Owner	18				500	0	0
" 7	" Sundry Sales — Woodlands	5				1	10	0
" 9	" Estate Improvement Buildings & Repairs Co. Loan	6				1866	0	0
" 10	" Cottage Rental ½ Year — Rents	16				87	0	0
" 20	" Hampion Bros Rep — Home Farm	11				45	6	0
" 21	" Comax, W. Pheasants — Sporting	4	1	15	0			
"	" " Hares	4	1	14	0	3	9	0
" 28	" " Partridges	4				3	0	0

Payments

Date	Voucher No.	Particulars	Ledger Fo.	£	s	d	£	s	d
1934 Jan 1	Pc	By Petty Cash	Pc				10	0	0
	£6	" Smith & Co Contract Building & Repairs, for new buildings	6				1866	0	0
" 2		" Floating Cash — Head Keeper	12	10	0	0			
		Farm Bailiff	12	20	0	0			
		Foreman — Woodlands	12	10	0	0			
		" — Work Yard & Repairs	12	20	0	0	60	0	0
" 7		" Weekly Wages — Home Farm	11	18	8	6			
		Woodlands	5	8	10	0			
		Buildings & Repairs	6	10	0	0			
		Works	7	6	0	0			
		Timber Yard	4	9	0	0			
		Sporting	15	25	10	0			
		Mansion	15				77	8	6
" 10		" King & Son Coal	15				58	10	0
" 12		" Corey & Co Petrol	15				10	15	0
" 14		" Brown, White, etc	15				6	6	0
		" Inland Revenue, Jones Sch A & B — Rates & Taxes	1				557	9	0
" 17		" Weekly Wages — Home Farm	11	19	5	0			
		Woodlands	5	7	10	0			
		Buildings & Repairs	6	10	0	0			
		Repairs Works	7	6	0	0			
		Timber Yard	4	9	0	0			
		Sporting	15	25	10	0	77	5	0
		" Wood, J. Woodruff — Home Farm / Works & Co / Timber Yard	11				58	10	0
		" Yarrow & Co Sundries	7				31	15	0
" 20		" Post Office Stamps — Insurance	3				10	0	0

at frequent intervals—not less than once monthly—by finding the balance shown by each of them. At the close of the financial year the balance of the Cash Book will agree with the balance of the passbook, though a Reconciliation statement (see p. 21) may sometimes be needed to allow for cheques drawn a day or two before the end of the year which have not been presented for payment at the bank, and for cheques paid in but not credited before the balance of the bank account is struck.

Floating Cash Account. Besides the Cash Book, a special cash account is essential in estate book-keeping to record the cash required by the heads of departments—the Bailiff of the Home Farm, the Head Woodman, the Head Keeper, the Clerk of Works—for wages and various expenses. This is called the Floating Cash Account. A cheque is drawn for a round sum sufficient to give each of these men the money to cover one week's payments. At the end of the next and of every subsequent week, each head is given a cheque *for the exact amount of his weekly payments*, and these are charged to the departmental ledger accounts concerned. Thus, each foreman begins every week with the original sum in hand. For example, if the Farm Bailiff is given £20 of Floating Cash on January 1st and spends £18. 8s. 6d. on farm wages and petty expenses, a cheque for this amount is drawn by the agent and given to the Bailiff to cash (see p. 15, Jan. 7). This brings his Floating Cash in hand up to £20 again.

Ledger. Simultaneously with the entry of receipts and payments in the Cash Book, the respective amounts are posted to their appropriate accounts in the *Ledger*. As with the Cash Book, any standard form of Ledger can be employed. In general, it should provide, on both debit and credit sides, columns for the date of each transaction; for the reference to the Cash Book or other Ledger account from which the transaction is posted; for the folio reference in the Cash Book or other Ledger account; and money columns for the amount of the transaction. Examples of Ledger accounts kept in this way are given on pages 7 and 9.

Floating Cash Account

Dr. Date	Jo.	£	s	d	Cr. Date	Jo.	£	s	d
1934 Jan 1 To Cash Head-keeper	C.B.2	10	0	0	1934 Dec 31 By Balance c/d	C.19	60	0	0
" " Farm-bailiff	"	20	0	0					
" " Foreman: Woodlands	"	10	0	0					
" " " Works Yard & Repairs	"	20	0	0					
		60	0	0			60	0	0
1935 To Balance b/d		60	0	0					

Woodlands Account

Dr.

Date	Jo.	Wages £ s d	Trees £ s d	Materials £ s d	Nursery £ s d	Total £ s d
1934 Jan 7 To Cash	C.B.2	8 10 0				8 10 0
" 14	.	7 10 0				7 10 0
Feb 1	.		10 0 0		5 15 0	15 15 0
" 6	.			3 2 6		3 2 6
Mar–Dec Other items	4	346 0 0		24 15 0		370 15 0
		362 0 0	10 0 0	27 17 6	5 15 0	405 12 6
Dec 31 Balance to Revenue & Expenditure a/c	C.17					74 10 0
						480 2 6

Cr.

Date	Jo.	Round Timber £ s d	Bark £ s d	Underwood &c £ s d	Total £ s d
1934 Jan 7 By Cash	C.B.1	70 0 0	15 0 0	1 10 0	1 10 0
May 1 "	"	30 0 0			85 0 0
"	.				30 0 0
June–Dec " Other items	. 3	200 0 0	20 0 0	40 5 0	260 5 0
Dec 31 " Works Yard	J	50 0 0		16 5 0	66 5 0
" Sundry Debtors	J	30 10 0		6 12 6	37 2 6
		380 10 0	35 0 0	64 12 6	480 2 6

In most Ledger accounts, however, it is necessary to know more than this, and the ledger must be large enough to admit of an analysis of the various items appearing in its accounts so as to give the detailed information necessary in the administration of the estate without any further abstracting. There must, therefore, be as many money columns as may be needed to tell the owner and the agent, at a glance, how the expenditure and the receipts in any department are subdivided under various heads.

The "Woodlands Account" on page 7 furnishes a good example. It is not sufficient to know that the Total Expenditure has been £405. 12s. 6d., and the Total Receipts £480. 2s. 6d., showing a surplus on the Woods of £74. 10s. 0d. It is necessary, also, to know how these totals are made up; and thus the expenditure is subdivided into Wages, Trees, Materials, Nursery; whilst the receipts are split up into Round Timber, Bark, Underwood, etc. The exact form of this subdivision will vary, and will depend upon the nature of the woodlands and the purposes for which they are being used; the headings suggested here are by way of illustration of that which should be aimed at. Another example is provided by the "Buildings and Repairs Account" on page 9. Here the headings of the analysis columns are arranged so as to provide information as to the distribution of the expenditure, with special reference to maintenance claims in respect of income tax recovery.

The number of Ledger accounts required depends, of course, upon circumstances; the ones figuring in the examples given later (pp. 25–30) are typical of those which will be needed on any ordinary country estate, but some of them may be found superfluous whilst others not included here may need to be added.

The whole process, then, in its simplified form, consists in entering all receipts and payments in the Cash Book, and in posting them from the Cash Book to their appropriate Ledger accounts, always making a sufficient analysis of the figures to supply essential information for efficient estate administration without the need for any further figuring. At the end of the

Buildings and Repairs Account

Dr. Date 1934		Fo.	Mansion £ s d	Farms £ s d	Cottages £ s d	Other Houses £ s d	Total £ s d
Jan 1	To Cash	C.B.32		1000 0 0	866 0 0		1866 0 0
" 7	" Wages	"		5 0 0	5 0 0		10 0 0
" 14	" "	"	3 0 0	5 0 0	2 0 0		10 0 0
Feb–Dec	" "	" 4	32 0 0	340 0 0	75 0 0	25 10 0	472 10 0
Dec 31	" Work Yard %	C.7	56 0 0	355 0 0	132 10 0	88 5 0	631 15 0
	" Farm Rents	J		145 10 0			145 10 0
			91 0 0	1850 10 0	1080 10 0	113 15 0	3135 15 0

Cr. Date 1934		Fo.	£ s d
Jan 9	By Cash	C.B.	1866 0 0
Dec 31	" Balance to Revenue & Expenditure %	C.17	1269 15 0
			3135 15 0

Revenue and Expenditure Account

Dr. Date 1934		Fo.	£ s d
Dec 31	To Rates & Taxes	1	2026 4 0
	" Tithes & Corn Rents	2	150 0 0
	" Insurance	3	230 10 0
	" Buildings & Repairs	6	1269 15 0
	" Management	8	636 10 6
	" Improvement Rent Charges	9	151 2 0
	" Estate Charges	10	137 10 0
	" Balance to Owner's % (being net estate revenue)		3313 2 6
			7914 14 0

Cr. Date 1934		Fo.	£ s d
Dec 31	By Woodlands	5	74 10 0
	" Home Farm	11	166 7 0
	" Rents	16	7673 17 0
			7914 14 0

Petty Cash Book

Dr — Receipts

Date	Particulars	No.	£	s	d
1934		C.B			
Jan. 1	To Cash	2	10	0	0
Jan.–Dec.	" Other Items	" 4	130	0	0
			140	0	0
1935	To Balance b/d		3	9	6

Cr — Payments

Date	Particulars	No.	Office Wages			Stamps & Telegrams			Travelling			Sundries			Total		
			£	s	d	£	s	d	£	s	d	£	s	d	£	s	d
1934																	
Jan. 2	By Stamps					1	0	0							1	0	0
" 4	" Telegram						1	3								1	3
" 6	" Carrier													9			9
" 7	" Carter, J.		1	19	7										1	19	7
Jan.–Dec.	" Other Items	L.8	99	18	9	8	4	0	22	5	2	3	1	0	133	8	11
			101	18	4	9	5	3	22	5	2	3	1	9	136	10	6
Dec. 31	" Balance c/d	L.19													3	9	6
															140	0	0

year the Ledger accounts are closed, and their balances, representing excess of income over expenditure, in accounts such as "Rents" and (possibly) "Woodlands", or *vice versa* in accounts such as "Management", and "Buildings and Repairs", are carried to a "Revenue and Expenditure Account" in the Ledger (see p. 9). On the *debit* side of this account appear the balances of all accounts showing an excess of expenditure over income; on the *credit* side appear the balances of those showing an excess of income over expenditure. The balance of the "Revenue and Expenditure Account" itself shows the net income of the estate available for the owner or the tenant-for-life.

This completes the description of the fundamental books required by this system in its simplest form. However, it will be found useful and even necessary, almost invariably, to employ certain books and records in addition to those comprised in Cash Book, Floating Cash and Ledger.

Petty Cash. It is inconvenient to overload the Cash Book with small cash disbursements, and so a *Petty Cash Book* is kept to deal with payments of this kind. It is fed from time to time as required by cheques drawn on the bank and entered on the "payments" side in the Cash Book, and on the "receipts" side in the Petty Cash Book. The petty disbursements from day to day are then entered on the "payments" side of the book. These payments should be analysed under appropriate heads according to their nature; an example of this book appears on page 10.

Rentals. The same position arises in connection with the rents received. It is not convenient to enter these in detail in the Cash Book; in the first place, it tends to overload this book with small entries, and in the second place, it is not possible, in the Cash Book, to preserve a record of how the sums actually received from tenants are made up. There may be deductions from the total, nominally due, for landlord's property tax paid by the tenant; for land tax, if any; for remissions of rent, etc., and it is necessary to keep a record of them. This is done in a subsidiary book known as the

Farm Rental for the Half Year ending March 25, 1934.

Date	Name of Tenant	Arrears brought forward			Half year's Rent			Total			Property Tax			Land Tax			Other Allowances			Net Amount Due			At Audit			At other date			Allowance			Arrears carried forward			Remarks
		£	s	d	£	s	d	£	s	d	£	s	d	£	s	d	£	s	d	£	s	d	£	s	d	£	s	d	£	s	d	£	s	d	
1934 May 20	Fellows, H.	50	0	0	240	0	0	290	0	0	37	16	0	2	10	0				249	14	0	224	14	0	25	0	0							£25 paid June 15th
	Howes, J.				150	0	0	150	0	0	20	0	0	1	10	0	5	0	0	123	10	0	123	10	0										£5 allowed for a new shed
	Brook, W.	30	0	0	100	0	0	130	0	0	16	0	0	1	5	0				112	15	0	100	0	0							12	15	0	
	Other Tenants	175	0	0	3470	0	0	3645	0	0	473	10	0	30	5	0	140	10	0	3000	15	0	2733	15	0	147	0	0				120	0	0	£140·10·0 sundry repairs
		255	0	0	3960	0	0	4215	0	0	547	6	0	35	10	0	145	10	0	3486	14	0	3181	19	0	172	0	0				132	15	0	

Farm Rental for the Half Year ending Sept. 29, 1934.

Date	Name of Tenant	Arrears brought forward			Half year's Rent			Total			Property Tax			Land Tax			Other Allowances			Net Amount Due			At Audit			At other date			Allowance			Arrears carried forward			Remarks
1934 Nov 20	Fellows, H.				240	0	0	240	0	0	37	16	0							202	4	0	202	4	0										
	Howes, J.				150	0	0	150	0	0	20	0	0							130	0	0	100	0	0							30	0	0	
	Brook, W.	12	15	0	100	0	0	112	15	0	16	0	0							96	15	0	96	15	0										
	Other Tenants	120	0	0	3470	0	0	3590	0	0	473	10	0							3116	10	0	2816	10	0							300	0	0	
		132	15	0	3960	0	0	4092	15	0	547	6	0							3545	9	0	3215	9	0							330	0	0	

Cottage Rental for the Half Year ending March 25, 1934

Date	Name of Tenant	Arrears brought forward £ s d	½ Year's Rent due Xmas £ s d	½ Year's Rent due Lady Day £ s d	Total £ s d	Deductions £ s d	Net Amount due £ s d	Cash Received At Audit £ s d	Cash Received At other dates £ s d	Arrears carried forward £ s d	Remarks
1934											
May 20	Burrows, W.	1 0 0	2 0 0	2 0 0	5 0 0		5 0 0	2 10 0	2 0 0	10 0	£2 paid Jan.10th.
	Green, H.			2 0 0	2 0 0		2 0 0	2 0 0			Empty Xmas Quarter
	Boots, J.	10 0	2 0 0	2 0 0	4 10 0		4 10 0	2 0 0	2 10 0		£2.10.0 paid Jan.10th.
	Other Tenants	5 0 0	90 0 0	90 0 0	185 0 0	4 18 0	180 2 0	87 10 0	82 10 0	10 2 0	£82.10.0 paid Jan.10th. £4.18.0 Value of Garden produce on quilting
		6 10 0	94 0 0	96 0 0	196 10 0	4 18 0	191 12 0	94 0 0	87 0 0	10 12 0	

Cottage Rental for the Half Year ending Sept. 29, 1934

Date	Name of Tenant	Arrears brought forward £ s d	½ Year's Rent due Xmas £ s d	½ Year's Rent due Lady Day £ s d	Total £ s d	Deductions £ s d	Net Amount due £ s d	Cash Received At Audit £ s d	Cash Received At other dates £ s d	Arrears carried forward £ s d	Remarks
1934											
Nov. 20	Sundry Items	10 12 0	96 0 0	96 0 0	202 12 0		202 12 0	98 12 6	96 10 6	7 9 0	£96.10.6 paid July 10th.

Rental. There are various forms in which it may be kept, and the following is recommended as having been found satisfactory in practice:

(1) For farms and land (see p. 12).

(2) For cottages (see p. 13). This form is for an estate where cottage rents are payable quarterly, but included in one half-yearly account. For monthly or weekly rentals, appropriate alterations must be made.

Only the total net cash received at each rent audit is entered amongst the Receipts in the Cash Book, and is posted thence to the Rents Account in the Ledger; for all details as to the way in which these totals are made up, reference must be made to the Rentals. Arrears of rent received at odd times are recorded in the Rental and then entered in Cash Book and Ledger in the same way.

Home Farm. For the Home Farm, or for other farms in hand, separate books of account must be kept. These are not specified here, as there are many publications descriptive of book-keeping methods suited to the needs of these farms; it is sufficient to note that in the Estate Cash Book a bare entry of all Farm Receipts and Payments is made under the appropriate dates, and that these are transferred to a Farm Account in the Ledger without further explanation. For all details reference must be made to the separate Farm Accounts.*

A few other books subsidiary to the Cash Book and Ledger will also be found necessary, such as the *Journal* and books required by the Clerk of Works, the Head Woodman and the Head Keeper. The form and purpose of these will be described as they come up in the example of a year's accounts which follows.

---

* The following books on Farm Book-keeping may be recommended:
Financial Book-keeping:

(a) H. W. Kersey, *Farm Book-keeping*, Part II (Headley Bros., Ashford, Kent).

(b) J. Kirkwood, *Farm Book-keeping* (W. Green, London).
Cost Book-keeping:

(a) C. S. Orwin, *Farm Accounts* (Cambridge University Press), *Farming Costs* (Oxford University Press).

CHAPTER III

EXAMPLE OF ONE YEAR'S ESTATE ACCOUNTS

THE following are the transactions of a land agent for the year 1934 on an estate of about 6500 acres, including the Home Farm in hand:

		£	s.	d.
Jan. 1	Receives cash from the Owner	500	0	0
	The Estates Improvement Co. advances for a new buildings contract a loan of £1866 @ 5 % including Sinking Fund, repayable in half-yearly instalments in 20 years. This amount is paid to L. Smith, the Contractor			
	Draws a cheque for Petty Cash	10	0	0
	Draws a cheque for £60 for Floating Cash, which is disbursed as follows: Head Keeper, £10; Farm Bailiff, £20; Head Woodman, £10; Clerk of Works, £20			
,, 7	Draws for weekly wages a cheque for £77. 8s. 6d.; i.e. Home Farm £18. 8s. 6d.; Woodlands, £8. 10s. 0d.; Buildings and Repairs, £10; Works and Timber Yard, £6; Sporting, £9; Mansion, £25. 10s. 0d.			
	Receives Cash for Underwood	1	10	0
,, 10	Receives Cottage Rents for the quarter ending Xmas, 1933. See Cottage Rental	87	0	0
	Pays the following bills for the Mansion:			
	King & Son, for coal	58	10	0
	Lorey & Co., for petrol	10	15	0
	W. Brown, for oats	6	6	0
,, 14	Pays Inland Revenue, Taxes, Sch. A and B	557	9	6
	Draws a cheque for weekly wages for £77. 5s. 0d.; i.e. Home Farm, £19. 5s. 0d.; Woodlands, £7. 10s. 0d.; Buildings and Repairs, £10; Works and Timber Yard, £6; Sporting, £9; Mansion, £25. 10s. 0d.			
,, 17	Pays for foodstuffs for Home Farm ...	58	10	0
	Pays for sundries for Works and Timber Yard	31	15	0

			£	s.	d.
Jan. 20	Draws a cheque for Health Insurance stamps		10	0	0
	Receives from Campion Bros. for pigs ...		45	6	0
,, 21	W. Lomax sends a cheque for £3. 9s. 0d. for game; i.e. £1. 15s. 0d. for pheasants and £1. 14s. 0d. for hares				
,, 28	Ditto, for partridges		3	0	0
Feb. 1	Pays F. Wilson, for trees		15	15	0
,, 6	Pays West & Son, for tools		3	2	6
	Pays W. Brown, for maize...		7	0	0
Mar. 1	Pays the Royal Commercial Insurance Co. Fire Insurance Premiums		41	15	0
,, 15	Draws a cheque for Health Insurance stamps		20	0	0
,, 31	Pays self one quarter's salary to date ...		125	0	0
May 1	Wood & Co. send a cheque for £85; i.e. for oak timber, £70, and for bark, £15				
	Round & Son send a cheque for oak ...		30	0	0
,, 15	Pays Queen Anne's Bounty, half-year's tithe		62	10	0
,, 20	Pays Rate Collector, half-year's rates ...		175	5	0
	Receives Farm Rents for the half-year ending Lady Day. See Farm Rental ...		3181	19	0
	Receives Cottage Rents for the quarter ending Lady Day. See Cottage Rental		94	0	0
,, 25	Pays into Owner's Account		500	0	0
June 15	H. Fellows pays the balance of his rent ...		25	0	0
,, 30	Pays Estates Improvement Co. £76; i.e. half-year's interest and 1st instalment of principal				
	Pays M. Ashby, Quit Rents		10	8	6
	Pays Miss M. English, half-year's Jointure		50	0	0

The rest of the Cash Receipts and Payments during the remainder of the year need not be given in detail, as the foregoing are a fair sample of the whole. For the sake of brevity they have been summarised as follows:

Receipts:

		£	s.	d.
May 21 to June 30	Sundry Farm Tenants, payments after Rent Audit	147	0	0
July 10	Cottage Rents for quarter ending Midsummer	96	10	6
Nov. 20	Farm Rents for half-year ending Michaelmas	3215	9	0
	Cottage Rents for quarter ending Michaelmas	98	12	6

		£	s.	d.
Jan. to Dec.	Sundry sales from the Home Farm ...	1772	10	0
	Sundry receipts for game	135	2	6
	Sundry receipts for timber, etc. ...	260	5	0
Payments:				
Jan. to Dec.	Petty Cash	130	0	0
	Sundry bills for the Mansion... ...	1905	10	0
	Ditto, Home Farm	1555	5	6
	Ditto, Buildings and Repairs... ...	472	10	0
	Ditto, Works and Timber Yard ...	624	10	0
	Ditto, Sporting...	580	0	0
	Ditto, Woodlands	370	15	0
	Insurance Premiums	158	15	0
	Rates and Taxes	700	5	0
	Tithes and Corn Rents	87	10	0
Nov. 20	Owner's Account	500	0	0
Dec. 31	Self, three-quarters' salary	375	0	0
	Estates Improvement Co., £75. 2s. 0d.; i.e. half-year's interest and 2nd instalment of principal			
	Miss M. English, half-year's Jointure	50	0	0
	H. James, one year's interest on Mortgage	37	10	0

Note. All receipts are paid into the bank and all payments are made by cheque.

The Petty Cash payments are as follows:

		£	s.	d.
Jan. 2	Stamps	1	0	0
„ 4	Telegram		1	3
„ 6	Carrier			9
„ 7	F. Carter, clerk, one week's wages ...	1	19	7
Jan. to Dec.	Other petty cash payments during the year are summarised as follows:			

	£	s.	d.
Office wages	99	18	9
Stamps and telegrams ...	8	4	0
Travelling...	22	5	2
Sundries	3	1	0
	133	8	11

These are the year's transactions on the estate, and each one of them must be recorded in the Cash Book under its appropriate date. A specimen double page of the Cash Book, showing the entries for the first month, has already been given (see p. 5); in the pages following appear the complete

Receipts — Cash Book — Payments

Receipts

Date	Particulars	Ledger	Fo.	£	s	d	£	s	d
1934 Jan 1	To Owner, Cash advanced	Owner	18				500	0	0
" 7	" Sundry Sales	Woodlands	5				1	0	10
" 9	" Estate Improvement Co. Loan	Buildings & Repairs							
" 10	" Cottage Rental ½ year	Rents	6				1866	0	0
" 20	" Cumplow Bros. Pigs	Home Farm	16				87	0	0
" 21	" Comax. W. Pheasants	Sporting	11				45	6	0
"	" Hares	"	4	1	15	0			
" 28	" " Partridge	Woodlands	4	1	14	0			
May 1	" Wood & Co. Oak	"	5				3	9	0
"	" Bark	"					3	0	0
"	" Round & Son. Oak	Rents	5	70	0	0	85	0	0
" 20	" Farm Rental ½ year	"	16	15	0	0	30	0	0
" 20	" Cottage Rental ½ year	"	16				3181	19	0
							94	0	0
	Forward						5897	4	0

Payments

Voucher No.	Date	Particulars	Ledger	Fo.	£	s	d	£	s	d
1	1934 Jan 1	By Petty Cash	Buildings & Repairs					10	0	0
		" Smith L. Contract for new buildings	"	6				1866	0	0
	" 2	" Floating Cash	Head Keeper	12	10	0	0			
			Farm Bailiff	12	20	0	0			
			Foreman Woodlands	12	10	0	0			
			" Works yard & repairs	12	20	0	0	60	0	0
	" 7	" Wages & Sundries	Home Farm	11	18	8	6			
			Woodlands	5	8	10	0			
			Buildings & Repairs	6	10	0	0			
			Works & Timber Yard	7	6	0	0			
			Sporting	4	9	0	0			
			Mansion	15	25	10	0			
2	" 10	" King & Son. Coal	Rates & Taxes	15				77	8	6
3	" 12	" Lorey & Co. Peat	Home Farm	15				58	10	0
4	" 14	" Bepium, W. Oats, etc.	Woodlands	15				10	15	6
5		" Inland Revenue, Taxes (Sch. A & B)	Buildings & Repairs	1				6	6	0
		" Weekly Wages	Works & Timber Yard	11				537	9	6
6	" 17	" Woods & Co. Foodstuffs	Home Farm	11				77	5	0
7		" Yarrow & Co. Sundries	Works & Timber Yard	7				58	10	0
8	Feb 1	" Post Office, Stamps	Insurance	3				31	15	0
9	" 6	" Wilson, F. Iron, etc.	Woodlands	5				10	15	0
10		" West & Son. Tools	"	5				15	15	0
11	Mar 1	" Brown, W. Maize	Sporting	4				3	2	0
		" Royal Commercial Insurance & Fire Insurance	Insurance					7	0	0
	" 15	" Post Office, Stamps	Management	3				41	15	0
12	" 31	" Agent. ¼ years Salary	"	3				20	0	0
13	May 1	" G. A. Bounty ½ years Tithe	Tithes & Corn Rents	8				125	10	0
14	" 20	" Rate Collector ½ years Rate	Rates & Taxes	2				62	10	0
	" 25	" Owner, Cash	Owner	1				175	5	0
				18				300	0	0
		Forward						3774	6	6

Cash Book

Receipts.

Date	Particulars	Ledger f/o	f/o	£	s	d	£	s	d
1934		Forward							
June 15	To Fellows, N. ½ year	Rents	16				5897	4	0
May 21	" Sundry Farm Tenants	"	"				25	0	0
June 30	" Cottage Rental ½ year	"	"				147	0	0
July 10	" Farm Rental ½ year	"	"				96	10	6
Nov. 20	" Cottage Rental ½ year	"	"				3215	9	0
Jan–Dec	" Sundry Persons	Home Farm	11				98	12	6
	"	Sporting	4				1772	10	0
	"	Woodlands	5				135	2	0
							260	5	0
							11647	13	6
1935									
Jan. 1	" Balance b/d						114	6	0

Payments

Ledger f/o	f/o	£	s	d	Particulars	Voucher No.	Date	£	s	d
Forward							1934	3774	6	6
Improvement Rent Charge	9				By Estate Improvement Co ½ year's Interest @ 1d.	15	June 30	76	0	0
					" instalment of Principal					
Rates & Taxes	1				" Ashby, M. Quit Rents	16		10	8	6
Estate Charge	10				" English, Miss M. ½ years jointure	17		50	0	0
Mansion	f.1				" Petty Cash		Jan–Dec	130	0	0
Home Farm	15				" Sundry Persons			1905	10	0
Buildings & Repairs	11				"			1555	5	6
Works & Timber Yard	6				"			472	10	0
Sporting	7				"			624	10	0
Woodlands	4				"			580	0	0
Insurance	5				"			370	15	0
Rates & Taxes	3				"			158	15	0
Tithes & Rent	1				"			700	5	0
Owner	2				" Owner, cash			87	10	0
Management	18				" Agent, ½ years Salary	18		500	0	0
Improvement Rent Charge	8				" Estate Improvement Co ½ years interest & 2nd	19		375	0	0
					" instalment of Principal					
Rent Charge	9				" English, Miss M. ½ years jointure	20	Nov. 20	75	2	0
Estate Charge	10				" James, R. 1 years interest on Mortgage	21	Dec. 24	50	0	0
Estate Charge	f.19				" Balance c/d			37	10	0
								114	6	6
								11647	13	6

entries for the whole year. The entries, both of Receipts and Payments, are for the most part self-explanatory. It should be pointed out, however, that the first entry appearing in the example, "Jan. 1. Receives Cash from the Owner...£500", will only appear where a new Agent has been appointed and is starting his work. He will need funds for carrying on the estate until his first Rent Audit. For the second and subsequent years, he will retain from the estate receipts a sufficient sum at the end of the year for these purposes, and the entry in the Cash Book on each January 1st will then read "Balance brought forward, being cash in hand." (In the example, this balance is £114. 6s. 0d.)

Receipts. Dealing first of all with Receipts, it will be noted that the date of the transaction is recorded first, and this is followed by such particulars as are needed to make possible an adequate analysis of it. Thus, under date January 21st, the receipt of £3. 9s. 0d. for game from W. Lomax is divided into two items, Pheasants £1. 15s. 0d. and Hares £1. 14s. 0d., so that these details may be accounted for separately in the Sporting Account in the Ledger (No. 4, p. 25) under the analysis of "Game" and "Ground Game" respectively. Again, the item under May 1st, recording the receipt from Wood & Co. of £85, is divided into its components, £70 for oak timber and £15 for bark, to admit of separate entries, under the analysis of "Round Timber" and "Bark" in the Woodlands Account in the Ledger (No. 5, p. 26). The analysis adopted is merely by way of illustration of what can be done in this direction; some agents might prefer further to split up "Ground Game" into "Rabbits" and "Hares"; some might like to sub-divide "Round Timber" into "Hardwoods" and "Softwoods". There is practically no limit to what can be done in this direction to meet the requirements of any particular estate.

Following the particulars of the transaction comes the name of the account in the Ledger to which it belongs, and the number of the Ledger folio on which this account appears. Money columns for recording the amount of the transaction, both analysis and total, complete the page.

Payments. Turning now to the Payments, the date of the transaction is again entered first. Then follows a column for the "Voucher Number". For the sake of ready reference it is customary to number all vouchers consecutively before filing them, and any one of them can then be turned up quickly when necessary. This applies, of course, only to payments of accounts; cheques for petty cash (see January 1st) or for weekly wages (see January 7th) are not vouched in the same way, and no voucher number can be assigned to them. After this column follow others for detailed particulars of the payments, the name of the accounts in the Ledger to which they belong, the Ledger folios on which those accounts appear, and money columns for analysed and total statements of the amount disbursed, all of them being identical with those already described in connection with Receipts. Composite payments made by one cheque must be split up in the Cash Book, so that the details can be recorded in the appropriate accounts in the Ledger. For example, the weekly wages cheque drawn on January 7th comprises the wages to be entered in the Home Farm Account in the Ledger (No. 11, p. 27), the Woodlands Account (No. 5, p. 26), the Buildings and Repairs Account (No. 6, p. 26), the Works and Timber Yard Account (No. 7, p. 26), the Sporting Account (No. 4, p. 25), and the Mansion Account (No. 15, p. 29).

No further explanation of the form and uses of this Cash Book should be required; it can be adapted with a little thought and ingenuity to suit the circumstances of any estate.

At the close of the year, the Cash Book is balanced by casting up each side and adding to the smaller such a sum as will make it balance with the larger. This figure should agree with the balance shown in the bank passbook at the same date, unless, of course, there are any cheques drawn at the close of the year which have not been presented by the payees, or any estate receipts paid in which have not been credited. In such cases an agreement between the Cash Book and the passbook may be obtained by a Reconciliation Statement, thus:

			£	s.	d.
31 Dec. 1934.	Balance as per Cash Book		114	6	0
	Add cheque drawn and not presented		37	10	0
			151	16	0
	Deduct cheques paid in but not credited		40	5	0
	Balance as per Pass Book		111	11	0

At the same time, the Petty Cash Book (see p. 10) is balanced to show the amount of petty cash in the office at the close of the year.

Ledger Accounts. To turn, now, to the *Ledger.* After each transaction is entered in the Cash Book it should be posted at once to the appropriate account in the Ledger. Any standard form of Ledger will serve provided that it be large enough to allow of space for an analysis of the items posted to it. The columns required are for date, particulars, Cash Book folio reference, analysis of items and total amount. The use of the analysis columns has been explained already (see p. 8), and for the rest, the posting of the Ledger is merely routine.

Journal. When the Cash Book entries for the year have been posted, the Ledger accounts cannot be closed until certain additional entries have been made. Reference to the Farm Rental (see p. 12) shows that when paying their rents the tenants have been allowed to deduct certain sums for property and land taxes due by the landlord but paid by them on his behalf. The effect of this is to reduce the total amount of the rents appearing in the Rents Account (No. 16, p. 29) and, at the same time, to increase the total amount of the Rates and Taxes Account (No. 1, p. 25) by the same figure. Entries must therefore be made in these accounts, *debiting* Rates and Taxes and *crediting* Rents with the total amount for the year, which was £582. 16s. 0d., of which £35. 10s. 0d. was for land tax and £547. 6s. 0d. for property tax.

To keep track of these additional postings to Ledger accounts, which do not come through the Cash Book, a book

known as the *Journal* is opened. The entries being few in
number it need be only a small book, ruled with columns
for the date and particulars of the entry, a Ledger folio

Journal

Date	Particulars	C.F.	Dr. £	s	d	Cr £	s	d
1934								
Dec.31	Rates & Taxes a/c Dr.							
	Property Tax	1	547	6	0			
	Land "	1	35	10	0			
	to Farm Rents a/c	16				582	16	0
	See Farm Rental							
"	Buildings & Repairs a/c Dr.	6	145	10	0			
	to Farm Rents a/c	16				145	10	0
	See Farm Rental							
"	Works & Timber Yard a/c Dr.	7	66	5	0			
	to Woodlands a/c	5				66	5	0
	for Timber supplied							
"	Sundry Debtors a/c Dr.	13	37	2	6			
	to Woodlands a/c	5				37	2	6
"	Works & Timber Yard a/c Dr.							
	Bricks 30-0-0							
	Tiles 20-0-0							
	Drain Pipes 20-0-0	7	70	0	0			
	to Sundry Creditors a/c	14				70	0	0
	for Materials supplied							
"	Buildings & Repairs a/c Dr.							
	Mansion	6	56	0	0			
	Farms	6	355	0	0			
	Cottages	6	132	10	0			
	Other Houses	6	88	5	0			
	to Works & Timber Yard a/c	7				631	15	0
	for Materials supplied							
			1533	8	6	1533	8	6

column, and money columns. It is written up at the end of
the year to provide for transfers from one account to another.
The debiting of Rates and Taxes and crediting of Rents,
mentioned above, is a typical example of a *Journal* entry,
but there are others.

The Farm Rental also discloses the fact that deductions have been allowed from rents due by tenants to the amount of £145. 10s. 0d. in respect of landlord's repairs effected and paid for by them. This sum likewise must be *credited* to the Rents Account and *debited* to the Buildings and Repairs Account (No. 6, p. 26).

Again, by referring to the Head Woodman's Disposal book (see p. 38) it is found that timber to the value of £66. 5s. 0d. has been supplied to the estate Works and Timber Yard during the year; this must be *debited* to that account (No. 7, p. 26) and *credited* to the Woodlands Account (No. 5, p. 26). At the same time reference to the estate Invoice Book (see p. 39) shows that sales of timber to sundry purchasers, to the value of £37. 2s. 6d., have been made which still remain unpaid at the end of the financial year. These also must be *credited* to the Woodlands Account, and a new account entitled *Sundry Debtors Account* (No. 13, p. 28) must be opened in the Ledger, and *debited* with the same amount.

Continuing, there are found to be accounts owing at the close of the financial year for building materials as follows: bricks, £30; tiles, £20; and drain-pipes, £20. These items, amounting to £70, must be *debited* to the Works and Timber Yard Account (No. 7, p. 26) and a new account must be opened in the Ledger, under the title of *Sundry Creditors Account* (No. 14, p. 28), to which the items are *credited*.

Lastly, the charges for materials issued from the estate Works and Timber Yard for use in estate repairs (£631. 15s. 0d.) have to be *credited* to that account and *debited* to the Buildings and Repairs Account (No. 6, p. 26). For income tax recovery it is necessary to analyse these issues under various heads, and the keeping of a record to facilitate this is one of the duties of the estate Clerk of Works, or Yard Foreman.

The foregoing transactions when entered in the Journal appear as on page 23.

Closing the Accounts. When the Journal entries have been posted to their appropriate accounts in the Ledger, the closing of the Ledger can be completed. Taking the accounts

No.1. Rates and Taxes Account

Dr.

Date 1934		Jo.	Quit Rent £ s d	Local Rate £ s d	Land Tax £ s d	Property Tax £ s d	Total £ s d
May 14	To Cash	C.B.2	10 8 6	175 5 0	32 9 6	525 0 0	557 9 6
June 30	"	"		175 5 0			175 5 0
July Dec	" - Other items	"					10 8 6
Dec. 31	" - Rents %	"			35 10 0	525 0 0	700 5 0
						547 16 0	582 16 0
			10 8 6	350 10 0	67 19 6	1597 6	2026 4 0

Cr.

Date 1934		Jo.	£ s d
Dec. 31	By Balance to Revenue & Expenditure %	L.17	2026 4 0
			2026 4 0

No.2. Tithes and Corn Rents Account

Dr.

Date 1934		Jo.	Tithes £ s d	Corn Rents £ s d	Total £ s d
May 15	To Cash	C.B.2	62 10 0	25 0 0	87 10 0
July Dec	" - Other items	"	62 10 0		62 10 0
			125 0 0	25 0 0	150 0 0

Cr.

Date 1934		Jo.	£ s d
Dec. 31	By Balance to Revenue & Expenditure %	L.17	150 0 0
			150 0 0

No.3. Insurance Account

Dr.

Date 1934		Jo.	Fire £ s d	Accident £ s d	National Health £ s d	Total £ s d
Jan. 20	To Cash	C.B.2			10 0 0	10 0 0
Mar. 1	"	"	41 15 0		20 0 0	41 15 0
" 15	"	"			20 0 0	20 0 0
Apr-Dec	" - Other items	"		17 10 0	90 0 0	158 15 0
			93 0 0	17 10 0	120 0 0	230 10 0

Cr.

Date 1934		Jo.	£ s d
Dec. 31	By Balance to Revenue & Expenditure %	L.17	230 10 0
			230 10 0

No.4. Sporting Account

Dr.

Date 1934		Jo.	Wages £ s d	Food £ s d	Appliances £ s d	Sporting Fund £ s d	Total £ s d
Jan. 7	To Cash	C.B.2	9 0 0	7 0 0	15 0 0		9 0 0
" 14	"	"	9 0 0				9 0 0
Feb. 6	"	"					7 0 0
Mar.	" - Other items	"	290 0 0	275 0 0	15 0 0		580 0 0
			308 0 0	282 0 0	15 0 0		605 0 0

Cr.

Date 1934		Jo.	Eggs £ s d	Game £ s d	Ground Game £ s d	Total £ s d
Jan. 21	By Cash	C.B.1		1 15 0	1 14 0	3 9 0
" 28	"	"		3 0 0		3 0 0
" Sundry	" - Other items	" 3		35 5 0	99 17 6	135 2 6
Date	"	"		40 0 0	101 11 6	141 11 6
Dec. 31	" - Balance to Owners %	L.18				463 8 6
						605 0 0

No. 5. Woodlands Account

Dr.

Date	fo.	Wages £ s d	Trees £ s d	Materials £ s d	Nursery £ s d	Total £ s d
1934						
Jan. 7 To Cash	CB.2	8 10 0				8 10 0
" 14 "	"	7 10 0				7 10 0
Feb. 1 "	"				5 15 0	15 15 0
Mar/Dec "	"			3 2 6		3 2
" Other items	4	346 0 0	10 0 0	24 15 0	5 15 0	370 15 0
Dec. 31 "		362 0 0	10 0 0	27 17 6	5 15 0	405 12 6
" Balance to Revenue & Expenditure % L.17						74 10 0
						480 2 6

Cr.

Date	fo.	Round Timber £ s d	Bark £ s d	Underwood &c £ s d	Total £ s d
1934					
Jan. 7 By Cash	CB.1	70 0 0		1 0 10	1 0 10
May 1 "	"	30 0 0	15 0 0		85 0 0
June/Dec "	"	200 0 0	20 0 0		30 0 0
Dec. 31 " Other items Works Yard	3	50 0 0		40 5 0	260 5 0
" Sundry Debtors	J	30 10 0		16 5 0	66 5 0
J				6 12 0	37 2 6
		380 10 0	35 0 0	64 12 6	480 2 6

No. 6. Buildings and Repairs Account

Dr.

Date	fo.	Mansion £ s d	Farms £ s d	Cottages £ s d	Other Houses £ s d	Total £ s d
1934						
Jan. 1 To Cash	CB.2		1000 0 0	866 0 0		1866 0 0
" 7 " Wages	"	3 0 0	5 0 0	5 0 0		10 0 0
" 14 "	"	32 0 0	340 0 0	75 0 0	25 10 0	472 10 0
Feb/Dec " Works Yard %	4	56 0 0	355 0 0	132 10 0	88 5 0	631 15 0
Dec. 31 " Farm Rents	J		145 10 0			145 10 0
	J	91 0 0	1850 10 0	1080 10 0	113 15 0	3135 15 0

Cr.

Date	fo.	Total £ s d
1934		
Jan. 9 By Cash	CB.1	1866 0 0
Dec. 31 " Balance to Revenue & Expenditure % L.17		1269 15 0
		3135 15 0

No. 7. Works and Timber Yard Account

Dr.

Date	fo.	Wages £ s d	Sundries £ s d	Timber £ s d	Bricks, Tiles etc. £ s d	Total £ s d
1934						
Jan. 7 To Cash	CB.2	6 0 0		21 0 0	10 15 0	6 0 0
" 14 "	"	6 0 0		20 0 0	261 10 0	6 0 0
" 17 "	"				70 0 0	31 15 0
Feb/Dec "	4	290 0 0	53 0 0	66 5 0	"	624 10 0
Dec. 31 " £.Cr. Woodlands %	J					70 0 0
" Stock in hand		302 0 0	53 0 0	107 5 0	342 5 0	66 5 0
			68 10 0	20 0 0	84 5 0	804 10 0
						172 15 0

Cr.

Date	fo.	Mansion £ s d	Farms £ s d	Cottages £ s d	Other Houses £ s d	Total £ s d
1934						
Feb. 28 By Materials issued & wages paid as per Foreman's book		6 0 0	55 0 0	12 10 0	5 0 0	78 15 0
" ditto		50 0 0	300 0 0	120 0 0	83 0 0	553 0 0
Mar/Dec " Repairs %		56 0 0	355 0 0	132 10 0	88 5 0	631 15 0
Dec. 31 " Stock in hand %d	J					172 15 0
						804 10 0
1935						
Jan. 1 " Stock in hand						

No. 8. Management Account

Dr.

Date		Petty cash	Salaries	Total
1934		£ s d	£ s d	£ s d
Mar.31	To Cash CB.2		125 0 0	125 0 0
Dec.31	" " 4		375 0 0	375 0 0
Dec.31	" Petty cash Expenses PC.2	136 10 6		136 10 6
		136 10 6	500 0 0	636 10 6

Cr.

Date		Total
1934		£ s d
Dec.31	By Balance to Revenue & Expenditure % L.17	636 10 6
		636 10 6

No. 9. Improvement Rent Charges Account

Dr.

Date		Total
1934		£ s d
June30	To Cash CB.4	76 0 0
Dec.31	" "	75 2 0
		151 2 0

Cr.

Date		Total
1934		£ s d
Dec.31	By Balance to Revenue & Expenditure % L.17	151 2 0
		151 2 0

No. 10. Estate Charges Account

Dr.

Date		Jointures	Mortgage Interest	Total
1934		£ s d	£ s d	£ s d
June30	To Cash CB.4	50 0 0		50 0 0
Dec.31	" "	50 0 0		50 0 0
			37 10 0	37 10 0
		100 0 0	37 10 0	137 10 0

Cr.

Date		Total
1934		£ s d
Dec.31	By Balance to Revenue & Expenditure % L.17	137 10 0
		137 10 0

No. 11. Home Farm Account

Dr.

Date		Total
1934		£ s d
Jan.7	To Cash CB.2	18 8 6
" 14	" "	19 5 0
" 17	" "	58 10 0
Dec.	" Other items " 4	1555 5 0
Dec.31	" Balance to Revenue & Expenditure % L.17	166 7 0
		1817 16 0

Cr.

Date		Total
1934		£ s d
Jan.20	By Cash CB.1	45 6 0
Dec.	" Other items " 3	1772 10 0
		1817 16 0

No. 12. Floating Cash Account

Dr. Date		Fo.	£	s	d	Cr. Date		Fo.	£	s	d
1934 Jan. 1	To Joseph Head-Keeper	C.22	10	0	0	1934 Dec 31	By Balance %d	C.19	60	0	0
" "	" Farm Bailiff		20	0	0						
" "	" Foreman Woodlands										
" "	" Works Yard & Repairs		10	0	0.						
1935	" Balance %d		20	0	0						
			60	0	0				60	0	0

No. 13. Sundry Debtors Account

Dr. Date		Fo.	£	s	d	Cr. Date		Fo.	£	s	d
1934 Dec 31	To Woodlands	J	37	2	6	1934 Dec 31	By Balance %d	C.19	37	2	6
1935	" Balance %d		37	2	6						

No. 14. Sundry Creditors Account

Dr. Date		Fo.	£	s	d	Cr. Date		Fo.	£	s	d
1934 Dec 31	To Balance %d	C.19	70	0	0	1934 Dec 31	By Works & Timber Yard	J	70	0	0
			70	0	0	1935	" Balance %d		70	0	0

No. 15. Mansion Account

Dr. Date 1934		Jo.	House £ s d	Garage £ s d	Stable £ s d	Gardens £ s d	Total £ s d
Jan. 7	Joseph Wagg Coal	CB.2	5 0 0	7 0 0	5 0 0	8 10 0	25 10 0
" 10	Petrol	"	41 0 0	10 15 0	6 6 0	17 10 0	58 10 0
" 12	Oats & Bran	"					10 15 0
" 14	Wages	"					6 6 0
	Other items	"	5 0 0	7 0 0	5 0 0	8 10 0	25 10 0
Jan. Dec.		4	515 0 0	418 0 0	356 0 0	616 10 0	1905 10 0
			566 0 0	442 15 0	372 6 0	651 0 0	2032 1 0

Cr. Date 1934		Jo.	£ s d
Dec. 31	By Balance to Owner's %	C.18	2032 1 0
			2032 1 0

No. 16. Rents Account

Dr. Date 1934		Jo.	£ s d
Dec. 31	To Balance to Revenue & Expenditure %	L.17	7673 17 0
			7673 17 0

Cr. Date 1934		Jo.	Farms £ s d	Cottage £ s d	Total £ s d
Jan. 10	By Rent	£31	3181 19 0	87 0 0	87 0 0
May 20	"	"			3181 19 0
June 15	"	3	25 0 0	94 0 0	94 0 0
" 30	"	"			25 0 0
July 10	"	"	147 0 0		147 0 0
Oct. 20	"	"	3215 9 0	96 10 6	96 10 6
		J			3215 9 0
Dec. 31	Rates & Taxes	J	582 16 0	98 12 6	98 12 6
	Repairs		145 10 0		582 16 0
					145 10 0
			7297 14 0	376 3 0	7673 17 0

No. 17. Revenue and Expenditure Account

Dr. Date 1934		Jo.	£ s d
Dec. 31	To Rates & Taxes	C.1	2026 4 0
	Tithes & Crown Rents	2	150 0 0
	Insurance	3	230 10 0
	Repairs & Building	6	1269 15 0
	Management	8	636 10 6
	Improvement	9	151 2 0
	Rent Charge	10	137 10 0
	Estate Charge	18	3313 2 6
	Balance to Owners % (being net Estate Revenue)		
			7914 14 0

Cr. Date 1934		Jo.	£ s d
Dec. 31	By Woodlands	C.5	74 10 0
	Home Farm	11	166 7 0
	Rents	16	7673 17 0
			7914 14 0

No. 18. Owner's Account

Dr.

Date 1934		Jo	£	s	d
May 25	To Cash	C.R. 2	500	0	0
Nov 20		" 4	500	0	0
	" Sporting	C. 4	463	8	6
	" Mansion	" 15	2032	1	0
	" Balance %a	" 19	317	13	0
			3813	2	6

Cr.

Date 1934		Jo	£	s	d
Dec 31	By Cash Advances	C.R. 1	500	0	0
	" Revenue & Expenditure %	C. 17	3313	2	6
			3813	2	6
1935	" Balance %a		317	13	0

No. 19. Balance Account

Dr.

Date 1934		Jo	£	s	d
Dec 31	To Cash in Hand:-				
	At Bank	C.R. 3	114	6	0
	Petty Cash	P.C. 1	3	9	6
	Housing Cash	C. 12	60	0	0
			177	15	6
	" Works Timber	C. 7	172	15	0
	" Yard Valuation		37	2	6
	" Sundry Debtors	C. 13	387	13	0

Cr.

Date 1934		Jo	£	s	d
Dec 31	By Sundry Creditors	C. 14	70	0	0
	" Owner	C. 18	317	13	0
			387	13	0

as they appear, the *Rates and Taxes Account* (No. 1, p. 25) is cast up and balanced. It then discloses the total expenditure under this head, and also the division of it between quit-rents, local rates, land tax and property tax. The balance must now be transferred to the *debit* of the Revenue and Expenditure Account (No. 17, p. 29).

The *Tithes and Corn Rents Account* (No. 2, p. 25) is treated in the same way, as is also the *Insurance Account* (No. 3, p. 25).

In the case of the *Sporting Account* (No. 4, p. 25) there have been receipts as well as payments, which reduce the debit balance. The account differs also from the ones preceding it in that this balance is not a charge against Revenue and Expenditure but against the Owner. Sporting may be a source of revenue on estates where sporting rights are let, but when they are retained by the landlord, all expenditure incurred in excess of any income from the sale of game is a personal matter and must not be represented as part of the normal cost of estate upkeep. The balance of the Sporting Account is thus *debited* to the Owner's Account (No. 18, p. 30).

Woodlands Account (No. 5, p. 26) and *Buildings and Repairs Account* (No. 6, p. 26) are properly estate concerns and are balanced to Revenue and Expenditure. *Works and Timber Yard Account* (No. 7, p. 26), on the other hand, is really part of the Buildings and Repairs Account, which, for the sake of convenience, is kept separate from it. It is a stock account, and after the issues of materials throughout the year have been *debited* to Buildings and Repairs Account as already described (see p. 24) the balance of the account represents the cost or value of materials still in stock. This balance is neither revenue nor expenditure, and so it is carried forward to the *debit* of next year's Works and Timber Yard Account, as representing the goods on hand for use in the future. It is advisable to check the stocks in the yard from time to time to ascertain whether the materials shown in the account are, in fact, on hand.

The next four accounts, *Management* (No. 8, p. 27), *Improvement Rent Charges* (No. 9, p. 27), *Estate Charges* (No. 10,

p. 27) and the *Home Farm* (No. 11, p. 27), are quite straight-forward and are closed by balancing them to Revenue and Expenditure. *Floating Cash Account* (No. 12, p. 28) represents money in the hands of foremen as explained on page 6; the practice, which is known as the Imprest system, is a common one and consists in giving to each enough money to cover one week's wages for his department and any petty expenses he may be likely to incur. At the end of the week, when his account is made up, each foreman receives a cheque for the exact amount spent, and this is charged to the Ledger account kept for his department. Thus, each foreman starts each week with the same amount of cash in hand, and ends the year with it. (See page 35.) The total of the Floating Cash Account represents, therefore, money in hand, just as the balance of the Cash Book represents money in the bank, and the balance is carried forward to the *debit* of the next year's account.

Sundry Debtors Account (No. 13, p. 28) and *Sundry Creditors Account* (No. 14, p. 28) show the amounts due to and by the estate for invoices for goods unpaid at the close of the year. The balances of these accounts are therefore carried forward to the *debit* and *credit* (in either case) of the next year, and they will be automatically wiped out when the accounts are settled in the following year.

Mansion Account (No. 15, p. 29) resembles the Sporting Account in that it is not an estate expense but one that concerns the owner personally. It is closed, accordingly, by balancing it to the Owner's Account (No. 18, p. 30).

Rents Account (No. 16, p. 29) is obviously an estate matter, and the balance is credited to the *Revenue and Expenditure*. This account (No. 17, p. 29) now comes up itself. It has been *debited* with the balances of all the accounts showing an excess of payments over receipts, and *credited* with the balances of those where receipts exceed expenditure. Thus, the balance of this account is the net revenue of the whole estate for the year, and as this is the amount available for the owner's private expenditure, the Revenue and Expenditure Account is closed by *crediting* the Owner's Account with this sum— £3313. 2*s*. 6*d*. in the example under consideration. The

Owner's Account (No. 18, p. 30) has already been *debited* with sums expended by the estate on his behalf (i.e. upkeep of sporting and mansion) and with sums drawn by him from time to time for personal expenses. The balance found on closing the account, £317. 13*s*. 0*d*., is the sum still available for his use, and it is carried forward to his *credit* next year for him to draw against.

Balance Account. The *Revenue and Expenditure Account* and the *Owner's Account* show the final result of the year's book-keeping on the estate. Before leaving the description of technical details, however, it is desirable to show how the accuracy of the accounts may be checked. It will be remembered that certain of the accounts—the various cash accounts, the Works and Timber Yard, Sundry Debtors, Creditors and the Owner—showed balances outstanding which were carried forward to the following year. If the accounts are correct the total of the *credit* balances will equal the total of the *debit* balances, and so the *Balance Account* (No. 19, p. 30) is constructed by *debiting* it with all balances brought forward to the debit side of the various accounts and *crediting* it with those brought forward to the credit side and the totals should agree.

To conclude, a glance through the Ledger will indicate the value of the analysis of each account in furnishing information on all the financial details of estate management; particularly when it is remembered that there is practically no limit to the extent to which the analysis may be carried. The headings given in the example are intended merely to be suggestions, and it is open to everyone to vary them in any way to meet the requirements of any particular estate.

CHAPTER IV

SUBSIDIARY BOOKS AND RECORDS

CONSIDERATION of the books and accounts described in the foregoing pages will suggest at once that other books and records are needed, subsidiary to them, but essential. A glance at the Sporting Account (No. 4, p. 25) in the Ledger, for example, shows that on January 7th wages, etc., to the amount of £9 were paid. Where does this item come from, and what are the details of which it is made up? This information comes from books kept by the Head Keeper. Every head of a department, the Head Keeper, the Foreman Woodman, the Clerk of Works, the Head Gardener, etc., must keep a *Wages Book* and a *Cash Book*, although the two may be combined in one book if desired.

The *Wages Book* contains a simple list of the men employed in the department each week, with the amount of the wages payable to each entered against them. From the total weekly wages is deducted employees' insurance contributions.

Head Keeper's Wages Book
Week ending January 7th, 1934

	£	s.	d.
A. Smith	3	0	0
H. Rogers	2	0	0
J. Williams	2	0	0
C. Tomkins	1	10	0
	8	10	0
Less employees' Insurance contributions ...		3	0
	8	7	0

The *Cash Book* shows how much money the Head of the Department had in hand at the beginning of the week (see Floating Cash Account, No. 12, p. 28). On the payments side he enters the net amount paid to the men in his department, as shown by the Wages Book, together with any Petty Cash disbursements which he has had to make. The Cash Book is balanced every week and brought into the Estate Office, when he receives a cheque for the exact amount of the week's payments. Thus, the appropriate Ledger Account will be debited with the actual amount spent, and the Foreman (in this example, the Head Keeper) begins each week with the same amount of cash in hand.

Head Keeper's Cash Book

Receipts						Payments				
1934		Fo.	£	s.	d.		Fo.	£	s.	d.
Jan. 1	To Cash	C.B.	10	0	0	By Wages		8	7	0
						„ 78 Rats' tails @ 2d.			13	0
								9	0	0
						„ balance c/d.		1	0	0
			10	0	0			10	0	0
Jan. 7	To balance b/d.		1	0	0					
„ 8	„ cash	C.B.	9	0	0					

If it be preferred to have a combined *Wages and Cash Book,* the same form of Cash Book as that above will serve. The

Head Keeper's Combined Wages and Cash Book

Receipts						Payments					
1934		Fo.	£	s.	d.	1934		Fo.	£	s.	d.
Jan. 1	To Cash	C.B.	10	0	0	Jan. 7	By Wages				
							A. Smith		3	0	0
							H. Rogers		2	0	0
							J. Williams		2	0	0
							C. Tomkins		1	10	0
									8	10	0
							Less insurance			3	0
									8	7	0
							„ 78 Rats' tails @ 2d.			13	0
									9	0	0
							„ balance c/d.		1	0	0
			10	0	0				10	0	0
Jan. 7	To balance b/d.		1	0	0						
„ 8	„ cash	C.B.	9	0	0						

name of each workman, the wages paid to each and the deduction for employees' insurance contributions, are written down in detail amongst the payments, instead of using the Wages Book to supply one summarised figure for all these entries.

For small departments of the estate, the combined Wages and Cash account has obvious advantages, but for estates or departments in which the number of men employed is considerable a separate Wages Book is desirable.

Another book which should be kept by the Head Keeper is the *Game Disposal Book*. On the one side is entered the bag, whether secured at shoots, or by the keepers pot-hunting for the house, or by trappers, under the appropriate dates. On the other side is an account of the disposal of the game, i.e. to guns, to the house, gifts dispatched and consignments to the market. Sufficient columns should be provided to allow of separate headings for the various kinds of game*.

The other heads of departments are in the same position, and the Stud Groom, the Head Gardener, the Head Chauffeur, must have Wages and Cash Books like those of the Head Keeper. In some departments, however, more information is needed about the use of the labour employed if the wages item is to be properly analysed in the appropriate Ledger Account. Thus, the payments to the men employed by the Foreman Woodman may be analysed between "Woods", "Nursery" and "Fences" if it be desired to keep a separate record of these branches of the woodmen's work in the Ledger. A combined Wages and Cash Book is impossible when such an analysis is made, and the Woodman's Book will appear as on p. 37.

The Wages Book of the Clerk of Works must be analysed likewise, to correspond with the analysis of the Buildings and Repairs Account (No. 6, p. 26) in the Ledger. In the same way the analysis of labour in the Wages Book of the Foreman of the Works and Timber Yard must correspond to that of the Works and Timber Yard Account (No. 7, p. 26).

* No example is given here, as the requirements of sporting estates differ considerably, and the construction of the book presents no difficulty.

Any receipts by the Foreman of cash for sundry petty sales must be entered on the Receipts side of his Cash Book, together with a "contra" entry on the Payments side when the money is brought into the Estate Office. For example, the Foreman Woodman's Cash Book given below shows that he received, during the week, £1. 5s. 0d. for 100 faggots and 5s. for a Christmas Tree, the total, £1. 10s. 0d., being paid

Foreman Woodman's Wages Book

Week ending January 7th, 1934

Name	Total £ s. d.	Woods £ s. d.	Nursery £ s. d.	Fences £ s. d.
J. Thompson	2 5 0		2 5 0	
P. Hobbs	2 0 0	2 0 0		
S. Bunce	2 0 0	2 0 0		
T. Digby	1 10 0		1 10 0	
A. Darell	18 6			18 6
	8 13 6	4 0 0	3 15 0	18 6
Less insurance	3 6			
	8 10 0			

Foreman Woodman's Cash Book

	Receipts					*Payments*			
1934		Fo.	£ s. d.		1934		Fo.	£ s. d.	
Jan. 1	To Cash	C.B.	10 0 0		Jan. 7	By Wages		8 10 0	
„ 7	„ 100 faggots		1 5 0			„ Agent, see *contra*		1 10 0	
	„ Christmas Tree		5 0			„ balance c/d.		1 10 0	
			11 10 0					11 10 0	
Jan. 7	„ balance b/d.		1 10 0						
„ 8	„ cash	C.B.	8 10 0						

over to the agent and entered amongst the Foreman's payments. This practice should be invariable. The foreman should never retain for the payment of wages and other disbursements the cash received for petty sales.

But not all of the Foreman Woodman's sales will be for

cash. Except on estates on which timber is sold standing by auction, the greater part of the sales will be effected at an agreed price for a measured quantity of timber, either standing or fallen, and they must be invoiced to the purchasers, by the Estate Office, in the usual way. So, the Head Woodman or Forester must keep a *Timber Disposal Book*, which is a record of timber and woodland products sold to customers or delivered to the estate yard for use in buildings and repairs. From this record, which must be brought into the Estate Office weekly, customers' invoices are prepared, and particulars are got at the end of the year for timber used on the estate (see *Journal*, p. 23), in the form of an annual total, to be debited to the Works and Timber Yard Account.

Foreman Woodman's Disposal Book

1934		Cash £ s. d.	Credit £ s. d.
Jan. 1	Cash Sales:		
	100 faggots	1 5 0	
	Christmas Tree	5 0	
Apr. 7	Smith & Co., Lincoln		
	700 ft. ash @ 2s.		70 0 0
	H. Digby, Sheffield		
	5 tons Bark @ £3		15 0 0
May 4	Works and Timber Yard		
	152 ft. oak @ 1s.		7 12 0
	90 ft. larch @ 9d.		3 7 6

Other departmental heads may have to keep similar books of record. The foreman in charge of the Works and Timber Yard must have a book on the debit side of which he notes the quantities of all materials received into the yard, either from tradesmen (e.g. bricks, lime, ironmongery, etc.) or from other departments of the estate itself (e.g. sand, timber from woodlands, etc.). On the credit side of the book he records the issues of materials of all kinds for the various building and repair jobs in progress on the estate. Quantities only need be recorded by the foreman, the pricing being done in the estate office. This book is a check on tradesmen's invoices for goods supplied, and it facilitates the allocation of the cost of materials used in repairs to the various branches of the estate—the mansion, the farms, the cottages, etc. The rulings of this *Yard Book* can be varied to meet the needs of any estate, but in general they should agree with the form adopted for the analysis of the corresponding Ledger account, the Works and Timber Yard Account (No. 7, p. 26). The balance of the Works and Timber Yard Account, which is struck after crediting it with the cost of materials used on jobs, represents the value of stocks of materials on hand in the Yard at the close of the financial year. The book value, ascertained in this way, should be checked against the actual stocks, as a test of the accuracy of the Yard Foreman's issue records.

Reference has been made to the *Invoice Book*, a record of invoices rendered to purchasers of goods of various kinds sold off the estate—timber, sand and gravel, game, the produce of the home farm, etc. Two forms are in common use. The first resembles a large cheque book, the particulars of each sale being filled in on the counterfoil, for office reference, and then on the invoice itself, which is detached and sent to the customer. The second consists of an interleaved book, with perforated invoice forms on which the account is made out in pencil, while a carbon inserted below it provides an office duplicate. When payment is received, entries are made in the Cash Book and Ledger and the counterfoil or the carbon copy is marked "Paid". Accounts outstanding at the end of the year are journalised (see p. 23), for entry in the *Sundry Debtors Account*, and in the appropriate Ledger accounts.

Other subsidiary books will be needed on some estates besides those enumerated above. In these days, for example, the gardens are run, not uncommonly, for the market, and the Head Gardener will need a *Produce Disposal Book* and other records. No difficulty should be found in devising them, following the analogy of those described for other purposes, all of which are adaptable to individual needs.

All these examples of Foremen's books are simple, and suited to the capacity of any intelligent workman.

CHAPTER V

GRAPHIC ACCOUNTS

ESTATE accounts and records, kept as described in the foregoing pages, supply all the materials needed for a consideration of the year's estate management, while comparisons also may be made with this and preceding years. How much of the gross income is being absorbed by taxation, and is the tendency of this charge upwards or downwards? What is the ratio of the farm rental to the cost of farm maintenance? What are the comparative costs of home-raised and purchased nursery stock? How has the Profit and Loss Account of the Home Farm fared since the appointment of the new farm bailiff? These and many other pieces of information, some of it of direct value in shaping estate policy, and all of it interesting, are available in the books. But even so, some search may be necessary through a considerable number of books, and often it would be an advantage if some readier means of reference to comparative financial results in the different departments of the estate were available over a series of years. Particularly, perhaps, would these be of value to the landowner himself, for he may not have that familiarity with the technicalities of book-keeping which makes the estate accounts "as plain as print" to his professional advisers.

No better picture of the financial history of an estate can be drawn than by plotting the essential details year by year on graphs or charts. Studies of the changes in the rates of taxation, of the cost of repairs, of the income from farm rents, can be made at any time by a visit to the Estate Office and reference to the appropriate series of ledger accounts. But graphic records, in the form of curves added to year by year, can be kept by the landowner or the agent within the compass almost of a pocket book, and they give a vivid picture of the changing fortunes of the estate. In normal times and under a stabilised policy of management, variations in the charts from year to year would be small. At the same time, any changes that there may be, whether within or beyond the control of the owner or his agent, are disclosed at once, and they challenge attention in a way that mere figures recorded in ledger accounts may not. Notes on the graphs should be made, of course, to explain the more striking deviations from the normal, and the series will then provide a valuable historical record.

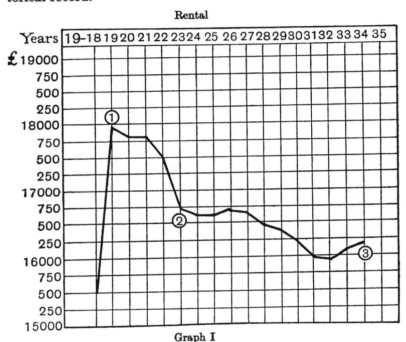

Rental

Graph I

① All farm rents raised 20 per cent. after the war.
② Abatements of farm rents following deflation.
③ Farms re-let at increased rents.

Four examples of graphic representations of estate accounts are given here. They are based upon the figures of a considerable property, corrected and extended the better to illustrate the graphic method. Graph I shows the Rental Account from the year 1918 to the year 1934, and it is a good example of the common experience in letting farms on a large estate. Rents had not been materially altered during the war, but in 1919 the tenants agreed to a rise of 20 per cent. as an alternative to the sale of the property. The graph shows, however, that the new values were held only for a few years. During 1922 and 1923, considerable abatements had to be made to assist the tenants, and through the rest of that

Property Tax

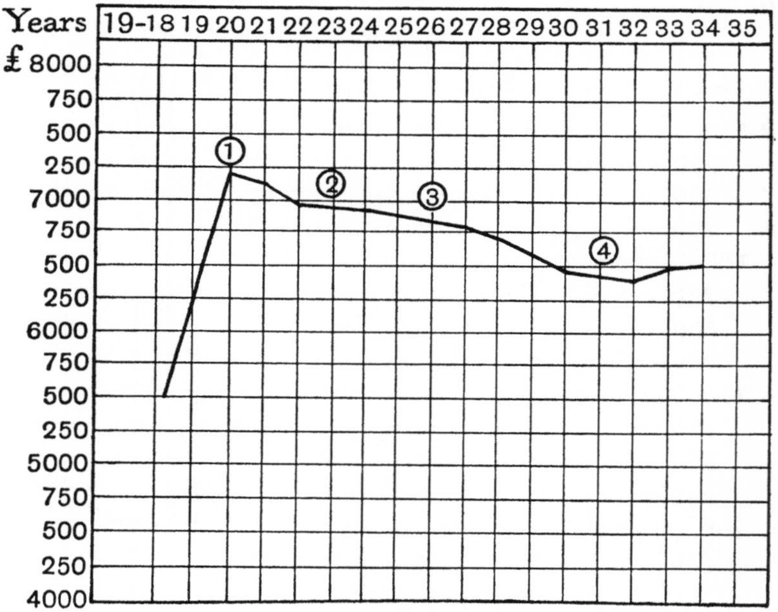

| Years | 19-18 19 20 21 22 23 24 25 26 27 28 29 30 31 32 33 34 35 |

£ 8000
750
500
250
7000
750
500
250
6000
750
500
250
5000
750
500
250
4000

Graph II

① Peak of war-time taxation and rental value.
② Income tax reduced to 5s.
③ Income tax reduced to 4s.
④ Income tax increased to 4s. 6d.

decade the tendency of rents generally was downward, until they were back almost to the 1918 level. Since then, the graph shows a slight improvement, due to the higher values which are obtainable now, under the influence of the new agricultural policy, when farms change hands.

The second graph illustrates the incidence of Property Tax. The jump to the peak of wartime taxation, when Income Tax was 6s. in the £ (1918/19–1921/22) is exaggerated, of course, by the increase of 20 per cent. in farm rents, which gave a larger taxable income. From that time the cost of taxation has shown a small but steady decline, as the rates of taxation were reduced and the rental declined, until the last year or two, when the improvement in agricultural conditions is again reflected.

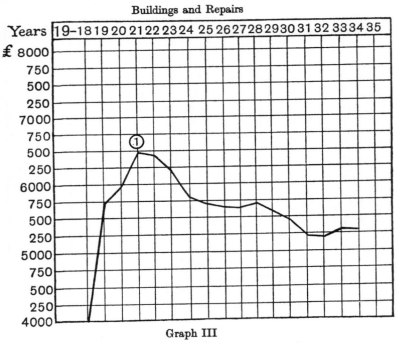

Graph III

① Increased expenditure 1919–23 due to war-time arrears.

As a third example, the Buildings and Repairs Account is given. It shows that the average expenditure on maintenance is about one-third of the Rental. It shows also how maintenance was perforce neglected during the war years, and the attempt to catch up the arrears in the next five years.

The fourth example of the graphic representation of accounts is that which shows the annual payments of interest and principal on loans incurred for estate improvements. This is a straightforward picture in which the lines run at the same level from year to year, rising only when new loans are contracted, and falling as old ones mature and are paid off.

Improvement Rent-charges

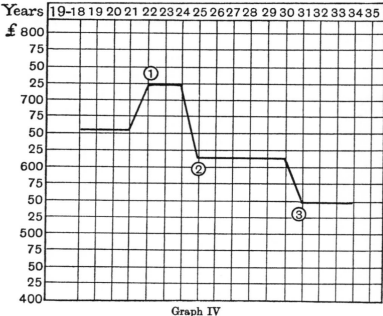

Graph IV

① Loan of £2000 effected, for cottage building.
② Loan for land drainage, effected in 1904, expired.
③ Loan for cottage building, effected in 1891, expired.

Similar graphs can be prepared for any of the estate accounts, but in practice it will be found hardly worth while to make them for any except the more important accounts of income and expenditure. They can be compiled in any estate office where there is a considerable run of estate books, and as the figures of succeeding years are plotted on the charts they give an increasingly vivid picture of the effect of changes of public policy, of changes in estate policy, of changes in economic conditions, on the fortunes of the landed industry.

INDEX

www.ingramcontent.com/pod-product-compliance
Ingram Content Group UK Ltd.
Pitfield, Milton Keynes, MK11 3LW, UK
UKHW042150280225
455719UK00001B/229